THE HIDDEN BEAUTY OF EVERYDAY LIFE

Also by Kent Nerburn

Simple Truths
Small Graces
Letters to My Son
Neither Wolf nor Dog
Make Me an Instrument of Your Peace
Chief Joseph & the Flight of the Nez Perce

Edited by Kent Nerburn

The Wisdom of the Native Americans
The Soul of an Indian

THE HIDDEN BEAUTY OF EVERYDAY LIFE

KENT NERBURN

NEW WORLD LIBRARY
NOVATO, CALIFORNIA

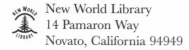 New World Library
14 Pamaron Way
Novato, California 94949

Text design and typography by Tona Pearce Myers

Library of Congress Cataloging-in-Publication Data
Nerburn, Kent, 1946–
The hidden beauty of everyday life / Kent Nerburn.
    p.   cm.
ISBN-13: 978-1-57731-530-8 (hardcover : alk. paper)
1. Spirituality. I. Title.
BL624.N47 2006
204'.32—dc22   2006000689

First printing, June 2006
ISBN-10: 1-57731-530-8
ISBN-13: 978-1-57731-530-8
Printed in Canada on acid-free, partially recycled paper

g A proud member of the Green Press Initiative

Distributed by Publishers Group West

10   9   8   7   6   5   4   3   2   1

To those who find God in the ordinary moments

Who know that life has meaning beyond the simple acts
that make up our ordinary days

Who show kindness in the face of hurt
Who seek the human in the eyes of those who have done them harm

Who offer consolation rather than judgment
Who offer help and hope rather than seeking their own advantage

Who feel the presence of God in the trees and the grasses
and a baby's helpless cries,
in the loneliness of the elderly, the love of young couples,
the good work of the laborer, in the silence of the night

Who are moved to tears by the kind act or caring word
Who stop to help the weak rather than seek the favor of the strong

I dedicate this book

May it find favor in your eyes

Anything we turn in the direction of God is a prayer.

— IGNATIUS LOYOLA

There is only one time when it is essential to awaken.
That time is now.

— GAUTAMA BUDDHA

CONTENTS

THE HIDDEN BEAUTY OF EVERYDAY LIFE

PROLOGUE:
SASKATCHEWAN WIND

A divine voice sings through all creation.

— TRADITIONAL JEWISH PRAYER

Years ago I was traveling across the great Saskatchewan prairies — a young man, alone, with a love of
the road and a dream in his heart. Evening was
approaching, and long shadows were darkening the
draws and stretching like fingers across the rolling
golden land.

A rancher, passing in a truck, saw me walking
and stopped to pick me up. Like many who live in

great spaces, he was a man of few words. We rode in peaceful silence until he noticed a break in the wire fence that ran along the side of the road.

"Got to check my stock," he said. "Want to come along?"

We walked to the top of a rise and looked out over the blowing amber grasslands. The sky above was fading to evening's lavender, and the wind hissed and sighed as it moved among the hills and draws and endless sea of tall prairie grasses.

The rancher turned to me and said a few words, but I could not make them out through the keening of the wind. I smiled and shrugged, and he went back to searching the distant hills for signs of his stock.

When we got back to the truck, I apologized for not understanding what he had said.

"Wasn't important," he said. "Just making conversation."

"It was the wind," I explained. "It was so loud I couldn't hear you."

He gave a short, knowing chuckle. "Oh, yeah, the wind," he said. "I don't even hear it anymore. The only time I notice it is when it stops."

We rode on in silence until we came to a rutted gravel turn off.

"This is my road," he said and pulled over to let me out.

I thanked him for the ride, we shook hands, and I stepped out onto the tiny ribbon of highway that moved, solitary, off toward the west.

How much, it seems, the voice of God in our lives is like that wind, so constant, so present, that we only notice it when it stops — in times of crisis, the loss of a loved one, a marriage gone bad, a fight with a friend that leaves us feeling misunderstood and unloved. Then we feel the great emptiness around us and reach out for the calming promise that we are not alone in the world.

But God's voice has not stopped. Like that great Saskatchewan wind, it has only paused to catch its breath, and to remind us by its silence to listen more closely, and take it less for granted when it begins to whisper once again.

This is a book for those who seek to hear that whisper — who believe that God speaks as surely in the murmurs of the trees and the laughter of the children as from the pulpits of the churches and the synagogues; who know that a mother tucking a child into bed is offering a prayer of joyful praise as surely as the cantor or the minister or the monk at evening vespers.

The great Hindu leader Mahatma Gandhi said, "It is better in prayer to have a heart without words than words without heart."

Jesus, in the Gospel of John, said, "The wind blows where it will, and you hear its sound, but know not from whence it comes or to where it is going."

This book is a reminder to keep our hearts open to the winds of God's whispers. It is not important that we know from whence they come or to where they are going, or even if we give them a name. All we need to know is that the moments of love, of caring, of the unprotected human heart, whenever we encounter them, are the voice of the spirit, blowing like the wind through our everyday lives.

Our task in life is to hear that voice, and to make of each day a prayer that bears witness to its presence.

DAWN'S
AWAKENING

The heart knows much that the mind cannot see.

THE SERMON
OF THE BIRDS

We recognize the spiritual in all creation,
and believe that we draw power from it.

— OHIYESA, DAKOTAH SIOUX

It is 5 A.M. on an early spring morning. I am in a garret on the third floor of one of the colleges at Oxford University in England. The early light of dawn is just beginning to cast a pale illumination on the pitched tile roofs and ancient church spires outside my window. I have gotten up to write because the birds awakened me. They love to nest among the overhangs and high stone chimneys of the red brick buildings of the college, and the promise of spring has brought them forth in full song.

The birdsong is different here, full of unfamiliar cadences and unfamiliar melodies. These birds are making different music than the birds outside my window in America, and this fills me with wonder.

I do not often stop to realize how different the music of nature is in each place on earth. But something about this birdsong makes me pause and take notice. It fills me, in a way far deeper than intellect, with a humble awareness of the beauty and mystery of the world around me.

Do they know each other? Are they talking to each other? Is their exuberance truly in their voices, or only in my hearing?

Does each mother know the chirp of her young, as each human mother can pick out the cry of her own infant from the voices of all others? Do they feel love?

These are the questions this birdsong calls forth in me. They lean me toward God and the ineffable mystery of life.

Our lives are filled with moments like these — ordinary moments when the hidden beauty of life breaks into our everyday awareness like an unbidden shaft of light. It is a brush with the sacred, a near occasion of grace.

Too often we are blind to these moments. We are busy with our daily obligations and too occupied with our comings and goings to surround our hearts with the quiet that is necessary to hear life's softer songs.

There is no shame in this. We are only human, and the demands of life make a raucous noise. But we must not let those demands drown out the quieter voices of the spirit. We must take the time to stop and listen, knowing that the voice of the spirit speaks more often in a whisper than a shout.

For spirituality is far more than religious practice. It is a cast of mind, a leaning of the heart, a willingness to see the shadow of the divine mystery in all people and all things. It is feeling the presence of God in every encounter, and seeing the reflection of the divine in the face of every person we meet on the street.

The Confucian philosopher Zou Shouyi said that we too often fail to recognize wisdom in those without talent, achievement, and fame. Jesus, in the Beatitudes, tells us to look to the meek, the poor in spirit, and the pure in heart. The Native Americans tell us to look at the elderly, because their lives have walked the long path toward wisdom.

They all are reminding us that the traces of the sacred are everywhere before our eyes, and that our task, as surely as performing acts of worship, is to find these sacred moments, hallow them with our attention, and raise them up as a celebration of the mystery of life.

The birds are quieting now. The traffic in the streets, the angle of the sun, or something more mystical and inexpressible has told them that they have sung enough.

But the silence they leave in their wake stays with me.

Like the fading echo of a church bell, they have lodged in my heart, and no church, no religious text, could do more than their gentle song to incline my heart toward God.

MORNING'S PROMISE

*The truest measure of our hearts
is how well we create love and hope
in the hearts of the children.*

JUST A KID

Their souls dwell in the house of tomorrow.

— KAHLIL GIBRAN

She is a sweet girl, not quite twelve, a flower just starting to bloom. I have known her since she was seven, though not well. I helped start the school she attends and have gone into her classroom once or twice a year to read to the students and talk about writing.

I always noticed her because there was such a look

of appreciation on her face. And it was not simply for me; it was for all of life. She was one of those rare children born with a sense of gratitude.

I used to cuff her playfully on the shoulder when I'd see her, asking, "How's my girl Sarah doing these days?" She would beam and blush, filled with pride at the attention she was receiving from an adult who seemed to inhabit a universe far more important than her own.

It was one day in the lunchroom, though, when our relationship really began to grow. I was there for a school-board function and was sitting at a table with a few of the teachers. Sarah came running up to me, at once excited and hesitant.

"Mr. Nerburn. Mr. Nerburn," she said. "I saw something you wrote in one of my books!"

She reached in her backpack and pulled out a dog-eared book containing a collection of inspirational thoughts for teenagers. I was pleased that she was reading it, and pleased that she had found the section I had authored.

"Would you autograph it for me?" she asked.

I signed my name and wrote a little note praising

her for her good-heartedness and concern for other people.

"Thanks for asking me, Sarah," I told her. "It's a real honor to have someone like you care about my writing."

She blushed and smiled, then ran off holding the book like it was the most precious object in the entire world.

From that moment forward Sarah and I had a special bond. Whenever I came into the school, she would come over to greet me. Whenever there was some display of projects, she would lead me over to look at hers.

It was one of those relationships that an adult cherishes, because you feel privileged that a child has chosen you as someone to value, and you know that your attentions can help give shape to a life.

As the time for her graduation from eighth grade approached, Sarah was required to give a public presentation about what she had learned and where she hoped to go in her life. Such presentations were held in the classroom at the end of the school day and were usually attended by only the parents and a few close friends. But when I heard that Sarah was going to speak, I knew I wanted to be there.

I took a place in the back of the room behind the smattering of family and relatives. When Sarah came in and saw me there, she broke into one of those blushes that made her freckles stand out like tiny stars. Her parents and grandparents she had expected; maybe an uncle or aunt. But Mr. Nerburn, the man who wrote books? Never.

Of course, she did just fine. She showed us her math papers and her artwork, and told of her work with her church youth group and of her dreams of doing something in the world to help other people. By the end there were few dry eyes, as much from pride in the flowering of such a beautiful young woman as from anything in particular that she had said.

I had brought her a gift — a signed and inscribed copy of one of my books. When her presentation was over and everyone had gathered around her to offer congratulations, I quietly handed her the book and prepared to leave. She was too much the center of attention to spend any time with me — and we probably wouldn't have had much to say anyway. But as I walked toward the door she pulled away from the well-wishers and came over to me.

"Thanks for coming, Mr. Nerburn," she said. Then, almost apologetically, she added, "And thanks for paying attention to me, even though I'm just a kid."

I gave her my usual cuff on the shoulder and a quick hug, then left her and her family to their moment of pride and celebration.

But her words lingered with me.

"Thanks for paying attention to me, even though I'm just a kid."

How little she knew; how little she understood.

Had it not been for her, those people would not have been gathered together. Had it not been for her freshness and promise, there would have been no tears. Yes, she was "just a kid." But that kid had brought us together and opened our hearts in a way no adult could ever have done.

I drove back home, wishing I could have found the words to tell her how special she really was. But the words were not there when I needed them — just the smile, the hug, and the playful cuff on the shoulder.

The following day I had to return to the school for a board meeting. I hoped I might see Sarah so I could tell her once again what a wonderful job she had done and what a special person she had become.

As I arrived, a group of kindergartners were playing in the schoolyard — running, screeching, chasing each other. I watched as one of them found a leaf and ran over to show it to her friends. Soon all the children were gathered around, pointing and jostling. I tried to see what it was they had discovered, but at my distance it appeared to be just a leaf. And, in fact, maybe that's all that it was.

At that moment, I realized what it was I had wanted to say to Sarah, what I wanted to say to all these children.

Never apologize for being "just a kid."

For you are the most important person in the world.

You are promise. You are possibility. You are hope when our hope has dimmed. You are joy when our hearts are heavy. In you we see the world as we dream that it could be.

Remain excited at the discovery of a leaf; it tells us there is still beauty in the small, when our eyes have gotten too focused on the great.

Play with each other on playgrounds; it shows us that all people of all backgrounds can meet each other with open hearts.

Keep talking to the dogs and the cats and the pigeons and the ducks; it reminds us that the spirit is present in all living things.

Keep laughing and giggling when you are surprised and delighted; it offers our ears the music of grace.

Do whatever it is that your heart would have you do. Laugh, cry, stomp your feet in anger, dawdle in the morning, resist bedtime at night. Allow us to see how important the moment is to you, and to share, for an instant, the importance of that moment.

For you remind us what it means to be alive.

You command us to be strong, you remind us to be gentle. In your eyes, we see the eyes of all children, and, for an instant, we understand what we have in common with all mothers and fathers at all times in all the places on the earth.

No, never apologize for being "just a kid." For you are strong beyond your wildest imagining. Your goodnight kiss can stop an army; your tears can melt the hardest heart.

For you have the gift of innocence. You have the gift of dreams. When we see you laughing and playing, our spirits take wing. When we lift you and hold you, we are consecrating a world of hope.

With these thoughts swirling, half formed, in my mind, I walked past the gaggle of children, past their squealing discussions and breathless examinations of the leaf.

Ahead, through the door, I could see the older students queuing up for lunch. Sarah would surely be there, and I would have a chance to speak with her again.

But then I changed my mind. I could see her far ahead of me, laughing with her friends, probably discussing boys and parties and plans for the weekend. She did not need me intruding upon her life. I was a part of yesterday. She was already living in tomorrow.

I continued up the stairs to the room where I would have my meeting. There I took my place at a circle of tables covered with folders and agendas and copies of minutes.

No, I thought, Sarah does not need me now, not

cutting in on her friends and quieting their laughter. She needs me here, helping the school — establishing policies and balancing books.

For we each have our jobs, she and I. Mine is to hold her safe in unseen hands. Hers is to be a mirror to my dreams.

The darkest waters hold the deepest truths.

THE BOY WHO WOULDN'T LEAVE

Blessed are the pure in heart, for they shall see God.

— MATTHEW 5:8

Last week I was sitting on a park bench, reading a book, taking in the rich, warm days of autumn. It was a quiet day, full of an easy peace, and I wanted to savor it in solitude. But a child kept moving around me, making noises, puttering, going back and forth.

I continued my reading and tried to ignore him, but the intrusion was getting irritating. There was no one else around, and this child seemed intent upon either annoying me or getting my attention.

Finally, a bit exasperated, I looked up and found myself staring into the face of a young boy about eight, straddling the bar of a dirt bike, staring back at me. He had a kind of indeterminate retardation that made me feel ashamed for my annoyance. His hair was black and stringy, his eyes wide apart, and his teeth crooked and ill-cared-for.

When he saw me looking, he grinned and waved. His movements were stiff and jerky, as if his muscles were a beat behind his intentions. But his look had the innocence of angels.

He said something to me, but it was unintelligible.

"Excuse me?" I said, hoping now to engage him in conversation, since he so clearly wanted my attention.

His eyes darted quickly. My inability to understand him had reinforced his sense of isolation.

"Nothing," he said clumsily, and looked down.

My mind raced back over the unintelligible syllables, trying to reconstruct them. There had been three, mumbled in a kind of singsong way that faded out at the end.

I took a chance. "Did you say, 'What's your name?'" I asked.

His grin opened like the sun. He waved his hand in ecstatic affirmation and nodded his head vigorously.

"It's Kent," I said.

He laughed, and nodded wildly.

"Kent," he repeated. "Kent."

Then he said it again, more quietly, savoring it as if it were some sort of magical incantation.

"My bike," he said proudly, pointing at the dented, rusty dirt bike he was riding. It was his pride, his self-worth, his closest and perhaps only friend.

I was about to ask him his name when he pushed on one of the pedals and went wobbling off down the sidewalk.

He circled once to make sure I was watching.

"Kent," he said, waving and watching. "Kent."

In his lonely world, he had made what passed for a friend.

I waved at him as he rode away, alone, down the street. I could hear him saying, "Kent," over and over, as if I had given him a gift of inestimable value.

I followed his progress as he churned on unsteady legs up the tree-lined street, then hopped the curb and skidded to a stop in front of a small, one-story house.

A woman was standing on the steps waiting for him. He ran up to her and put his arms around her.

She met his embrace with her own, and they stood there, mother and child, holding on to each other in the afternoon sun.

I thought of my own son, only a few years older than this boy, increasingly uncomfortable with his parents' touch as he seeks to separate and define himself in an autonomous adult world. How much would his mother and I give for a hug of this purity and innocence. How much do we dream of seeing him bounding up the steps and allowing us to gather him in our arms. But those days are gone. His love, now, is expressed mostly symbolically, and with more circumspection and caution.

I watched from my distant vantage point as the woman gently stroked her son's hair. He leaned against her, making no effort to pull away, resting in her embrace like a peaceful and weary child.

How lucky you are, I thought, to have a son who will never grow beyond childhood innocence. What a gift you have been given to know such guileless love.

They held their embrace for almost a minute. Then the mother bent down and kissed the boy on the forehead. She opened the door, and they walked together into the tiny, rundown house.

I sat back down, touched by what I had seen and

satisfied to return to my reading. But the image of the boy and his guileless smile would not leave me. The thought of the mother's gentle embrace filled me with warmth.

I shut my book and walked slowly down the block to the small house that the two of them had just entered. From the sidewalk I could see the mother standing by the sink in the kitchen. She was laughing and talking. The boy was walking back and forth in his jerky, clumsy way.

I thought of going to the door, of telling her how she and her son had touched me on this warm autumn afternoon. But it seemed intrusive.

I walked back down the street to my solitary park bench, leaving behind this house in which there was so much burden and so much love.

How little, I thought, do we understand of life's wondrous ways, and how hard it is to see the blessings in the shadows.

But there is wine like sunlight and there is wine like blood.

It does not matter which cup is passed to us. We must learn to consecrate life's gifts with love.

We are not called only to proclaim God
but to be the presence of God, reflected.

THE QUIET
MOTHER

God's name on one's lips is itself salvation.

— MAHATMA GANDHI

I overhear their conversation. It is hard to avoid. They are but a table away from me, and their voices are so impassioned. One woman is strong and certain. The other speaks more quietly and with less self-assurance. They are discussing the raising of children.

The confident woman is telling stories of her church and the activities they are doing. All seem good and honorable — serving food to the hungry, helping to build houses — the stuff of the Beatitudes, where, to my mind, Christianity finds its strongest voice.

It would be enough if she would leave it at that, but she does not. She is challenging her quieter friend, taking her to task for failing to give her children a properly religious upbringing.

The quieter woman hesitates, fumbling for words. "I think I'm a spiritual person," she says. "I believe in God. I try to teach my children what is right."

It is a heartfelt answer, but it lacks the bright certitude of the other woman's conviction. I would love to step in, to speak my piece, for I know the struggle she is facing.

She is a woman with a good heart. I can tell by the objects she carries — a bouquet of flowers, a box of thank-you notes. She understands the power of beauty, the need to show gratitude and thanks.

Perhaps she does not declare her religious beliefs as boldly as her more confident friend does, but I can feel their presence, and I am sure that her children, playing happily with toys in the children's corner of the coffee shop, can feel them as well. For she is one of the quiet believers — those who live a life of service, trying to shape their small corner of the world into a place of warmth and love by making each ordinary act of life a prayerful offering to the great mystery we know as "God."

And she is not alone.

There are many among us who believe in God but do not loudly proclaim our belief. We know that our minds are small vessels in which to hold so great a mystery. We believe, as the Bible says, that there are many rooms in our Father's mansion, and that all rooms are welcoming and all rooms are good. We do not wish to tell others that one room is greater than the others; we do not wish to leave anyone standing outside the door.

We want our children to be people of faith, but we do not wish them to be blinded by belief. We see our task as helping them find their place in God's mansion. We do not care which room they choose, only that it be a place alive with the sacredness of life, the kinship of all creatures, and the true conviction that we are each our brothers' and sisters' keeper.

If this is within the hallowed walls of a church and the embracing arms of a traditional faith, so be it. If it is on a starlit hillside, or in the touch of a lonely person's hand, so be that as well. We pass no judgment on how the spirit speaks, asking only that it speak in a voice of kindness and love.

I am reminded of the words of Chief Joseph when speaking to the Christian missionaries about his people's religion, "We do not quarrel about God. We do not want to learn that."

As I listen to these women, I pray that their children, playing so innocently amidst the books and toys, will not be forced to learn that.

For our children are but gifts that we are given, a moment's grace that we are asked to shape and share. We should raise them to be open to the world — full of faith, but not blind with belief; respectful of all who are honest seekers; and guided in their lives by a kind and caring heart.

Give them the language of God, for the words we use shape the world we see. If the words "God" and "spirit" and "sacred" and "holy" come easily to their lips, the meanings they contain will lodge easily in their hearts. They will be alive to the world of the unseen and will quietly open themselves to the mystery of life.

Give them the eyes of wonder. Show them, as best you are able, the beauty of everything in the universe — the stones, the trees, the birds, the people. Let them know that awe and humility, as surely as knowledge and understanding, are worthy paths to God.

Show them the connection, not the obligation, in their daily affairs. Let them see that the phone calls they make to grandmothers, and the thank-you notes they write to people they barely know, are really gossamer threads strung between hearts. Teach them that a life of service is a life of peace, and that a small faith can be as powerful as a large belief.

But I need not worry. These women are both seekers, one within the hallowed walls of the church, the other in the sacred fields of the heart.

Each, in her own way, will lead her children to God. For God lives as surely in the beauty of a flower as in the majesty of a cathedral.

Give a child the words to speak and the eyes to see, and the heart will find God as a traveler finds a pathway home.

DAY'S JOURNEY

The world we touch
is the world they made.
We stand upon their shoulders
as we stand upon the land.

MY FATHER'S TOOLBOX

Let the beauty we love be what we do.

— RUMI

A light switch in a closet is broken. The fix does not seem complicated, but I am no lover of electricity. It feels too potent, too unknown — I have seen too many cartoons of God shooting lightning bolts down on people from his finger.

But this broken light switch seems within my grasp. A screwdriver, a flashlight, something for stripping wires; I think I can handle it.

I make my way to the garage to look for the tools. The place is not in shambles, but it is close. I keep things roughly categorized — wrenches here, odd screws and bolts there, old license-plate brackets and floor mats over in the corner.

Several times a year I order and structure and label and box. But things quickly fall apart. A tool gets piled on a shelf because I need to grab another, some random object that does not fit into one of my predetermined categories gets left on a ledge to be filed away later, and soon the chaos has returned.

My father, unlike me, was an organized man. His garage looked like the back room of an old-time hardware store, with shelves of perfectly labeled boxes arranged in perfectly ordered rows. But when he died and we had to go through those boxes, we found that they contained used hinges, old brown electrical cords, miscellaneous doorknobs, ancient fuses, locks with no keys, keys with no locks, and all manner of strange paraphernalia, well labeled and well categorized, but of no conceivable use to anyone.

I seem to have inherited my father's tendency to save without the corresponding tendency to organize. So the same mysterious doorknobs and keyless locks can be found in my garage, but they are not in well-labeled boxes. They sit on shelves next to old paint rollers and spray cans and outmoded telephones that seemed too good to throw away. It makes for a frustrating experience when looking for something as simple as a screwdriver or a flashlight.

This is why the green metal toolbox is so important to me.

It came from my father. I can feel his presence, and the presence of his generation, in this toolbox. It is not forest green or some other designer hue meant to catch the eye of a passing shopper. It is a more industrial green — the kind of no-nonsense color that one might expect to see on heavy machinery roaring and rumbling on some factory floor.

It is a shade brighter than the olive drab of the military — in my father's day that color had a kind of cultural sacredness. You did not use it for any civilian purpose.

But this color was a near sibling to it. It spoke of a brotherhood of purpose — working together to build a better world.

The box has no lock. The two sides of the top simply fold over and lap against each other, forming an angled roof, like a miniature metal house.

It was made in the day when trust was a given

and the distinction between *mine* and *yours* was not so strong. It always makes me think of another man of my father's generation — a kind, tough old mailman who lived near me in the woods of Oregon — who, once he trusted me, had said, simply, "If there's anything you ever need, you just come and take it out of my shed." No sign-out sheets, no lectures about being sure to return it. That was all presumed.

This box presumes the same.

My father had been proud of this toolbox. It was the best you could get in his day. It was one of those objects that you achieved, working your way up to it from wooden boxes or cloth rolls. Once you obtained it, you did not expect to replace it. It had been made for the ages.

My father had not replaced it. On the contrary, he had claimed it. He had stenciled his name on it, LLOYD NERBURN. Over the years it has become scratched and faded. But it remains today. This is Lloyd Nerburn's toolbox. Kent Nerburn is only its inheritor, its caretaker.

I sometimes feel like I am violating its trust with my sloppiness, my failure to wipe tools clean when I am finished with them, my disinterest in keeping it organized. But this is just the echo of the sense I have that I am somehow violating his trust with the easy good fortune and more casual attitude I have toward my own life.

I don't work as hard as he did; I don't keep things as orderly in the family as he did; I don't make sure that everything is clean and returned to its proper place. My life is more managed chaos, like my garage, like the contents of the toolbox.

But this toolbox reminds me of where I have come from, and on whose shoulders I stand.

It is strange how this toolbox has become so important to me. It is not something my father would have thought to pass on to me. He was well aware of my sloppiness and lack of interest in home repairs. First would have been the autographed picture of Babe Ruth, signed for my grandmother by the great slugger when she had crossed paths with him in her job as a hotel elevator operator. But that photograph means little to me, because it meant little to my father. He valued it only because it was rare; he was anxious to pass it on only because he knew it had some financial value.

But the toolbox, he loved. It was a metaphor for

his dreams of family — an unbreakable little house, solid, ordered, containing the solution to life's uncertainties and problems, and protecting everything that lay within. Though he would never have thought about it in this way, it was a symbol of the hard-won success he had achieved in his rise from orphaned boy to husband and father and proud head of a family.

I love it now, too, because it meant so much to him. When I touch that toolbox, I can feel my father's hands.

Strange it is how little attention we pay to things of the heart. We think it is the financial inheritance that matters, or the family heirlooms, so carefully protected and hidden away. But we are known by the things that we love, and remembered for what we held dear. We use my wife's mother's silverware on special occasions, making passing mention of its heritage. But the little wooden boat of stuffed animals that caused her to giggle every time she saw it — that we look at almost daily, and always with a fondness that brings us close to tears.

I search around in the toolbox amidst the jostle of wrenches and pliers until I fish out a wire stripper and a screwdriver. They are both slippery with oil from some prior home repair misadventure, but they will do. I wipe them on a rag and head upstairs to do battle with the light switch.

Behind me, the toolbox sits, its lid open and its contents askew. My father would have closed it, wiped its handles clean, and placed it back on the shelf. But I am merely his son, I am not his better.

And as I climb the stairs, I can't help but wonder what it is my son will cherish when I am gone.

What object that I take for granted will be the memory by which I will be known?

What will he remember that I loved?

*We must find a way to replace yearning
for what life has withheld from us
with gratitude for what we have been given.*

KITE DANCER

*Once you have flown, you will walk the earth
with your eyes turned skyward.*

— LEONARDO DA VINCI

The sky above the park is alive with kites. It is a breezy spring day, and the children are out.

This is a rare occurrence, for kites live best where the spaces are great and the sky looms larger than the land, beckoning the children to look upward and send their dreams flying toward the heavens. Ours is a place of lakes and woods and deep winter snows. Children keep their eyes close to the earth, and send their dreams racing down rivulets of melting waters, or sliding across drifts, or skipping on stones across the shimmering surfaces of lakes.

But on rare days like this, when the sky is both gentle and playful, it calls to them and they take their kites to the open fields, the meadows, the parks, and the school yards and send them skyward to make a playmate of the winds.

Often they fail. These are not children practiced in arts of the sky, and their kites too often spin out of control, whip crazily in the wind, and plummet heavily to the earth. Other times they never leave the earth at all, bouncing fitfully on the ground behind as the children try to run them into the air on legs too short across fields too small.

But on this day, the winds are gentle and the sky is kind. The kites have risen, and the children stand at the ends of their strings, eyes skyward and attention rapt, mesmerized by this connection with the heavens that they can only dimly understand.

It reminds me of a day many years ago in a very different landscape under a very different sky.

It was 7:30 in the evening on a late spring day in Gallup, New Mexico. The sun was going down in a blaze of orange, turning the surrounding desert into a crucible of fire.

But I couldn't take time to look. I had gotten lost on a side street and was trying frantically to keep my eyes on the road while attempting to decipher the tiny red and blue lines on the map splayed open on my lap.

Louise was nodding off next to me, and Nik, still a young boy, was curled up in the back, deep in sleep. Though I could have used some help, it seemed better to let them rest.

But every turn took me farther from the main street. It seemed impossible. Gallup was little more than a strip town — a remnant of the once legendary Route 66, built to service the needs and hungers of a post-Depression nation traveling from Chicago to Los Angeles. Yet, every turn I took sent me to the edge of some arroyo or into another dusty dead-end street.

My irritation had been building all day. The looming power of Monument Valley and the awesome spiritual majesty of the high New Mexico desert had turned me in on myself, and the requests for toilet stops and questions about when we were going to eat or where we were going to stay seemed mundane and intrusive. I was feeling tethered to family and finitude, and it was making me quarrelsome.

Another dead end. Another street fading off into nowhere.

I slammed the car into reverse and roared off in the direction I had come, cursing everything the world had placed before me. I just wanted to get out — of Gallup, of myself, of my family, of my skin.

I raced around a corner, hoping that this was the turn that would get me back to the highway. But instead, I was blinded by a flash of orange light exploding across the windshield.

I jammed on my brakes and shielded my eyes, then eased the car to the side of the road to let my sight recover. All was a swirling blur of multicolored starbursts and flashes. I had turned directly west and, for the moment, my sight had been stolen from me by the blazing desert sun.

Then, as my eyes adjusted and the world came back into view, I saw him.

He was sitting alone in a wheelchair in the center of a dusty, windblown lot. Papers were tumbling past him on the hot desert wind, and small cyclones of sand rose up around him like furies. But he was still as stone. He sat there in that wheelchair like some great Egyptian temple god, hands in his lap, eyes cast skyward.

I watched him for a while, wondering if he needed help. No sane person would go out into that hot dusty lot to sit quietly in its center, buffeted by wind and cut by the sharp edges of burning blowing sand. I wondered if I should offer him assistance.

But then I noticed something. He was moving his hands ever so slightly as he stared into the majestic evening sky.

I followed his gaze upward toward the heavens. There, almost invisible, I could barely make out the small speck of a kite.

The man moved his hands slightly; the kite dipped and swooped. He moved them again and the kite raced upward. It seemed alive, like a spirit, like a dancer on the wind.

I was transfixed. This man was not an ordinary kite flier. He was an artist, a choreographer. In his hands, the kite moved like a song.

For a moment, I forgot my anger and frustration. I peered more closely, trying to get a sense of this man who could make a kite sing an anthem to the sun.

He had a shirt buttoned up to his collar and a shock of black hair hanging down over his forehead. He was Native American, or Mexican. He had a quiet, almost beatific smile. He had no legs.

Now, I am not a man who asks for miracles. I'm happy when the veil parts for a moment, offering me a glimpse of life's simple beauty. But this was as close to a miracle as I am likely to receive. Like Saul on his horse, God's light had blinded me and thrown me to earth. And like Saul, when my sight was restored, the world around me had been changed.

There before me was a man who was truly bound to the earth and finitude. His was not some illusion of entrapment, churned up in the cauldron of his own imagination. He was the very embodiment of limitation.

Yet while I drove across the great spaces of the West with a wonderful family at my side, complaining that my freedom was not large enough to contain the grandness of my spiritual yearnings, he was reduced to holding his freedom on a string and watching it perform a distant dance on the currents of the wind. Yet it was I who was feeling constrained, and he who was wearing the smile of peace.

I pulled the car into gear and moved slowly out toward the highway, feeling both shame and gratitude. The streets were suddenly not so confusing, the route out not so hard to divine.

I looked over at the man. He had not noticed me. He was too intent upon watching the kite as it dipped and bobbed and glinted against the blaze of setting sun.

I did not tell Louise. Her breathing was gentle. I did not wake Nik. We had miles to go across the growing desert night. But I kept that man in my heart, and he remains there today.

Like the innocent children, watching their kites on this wind-washed spring day, he had turned my eyes toward the heavens. And in drawing my gaze skyward, he had given me eyes to see the richness of my gifts here on earth.

Our life is a work of art.
We must seek always to be its artist.

SURPRISED
BY GOD

*God sometimes seems to speak to us most intimately
when he catches us, as it were, off our guard.*

— C. S. LEWIS

It was a warm day, sweltering and sweaty in that way
that only humid climates can produce. We were in
Florence, the great city of the Italian Renaissance, the
home of the Medicis, Michelangelo, Dante, Giotto.
To wander its streets is to feel the heavy presence of
greatness; to enter its museums is to stand in wonder
at the human capacity to create.

But it was the heat, not the art, that was controlling

our lives that day. Each step was an effort, each movement a chore. The shopkeepers, save those who made their living off tourists, had wisely shut down for the afternoon and gone home to rest. They would reopen later in the evening when the weather had cooled.

But for those of us on the street — the visitors and tourists — there was no shutting down, no respite. We were there to drink in the art and the culture, the smells and the sounds. We had come from all corners of the world to be part of the solid, muscular grace of this city. We did not wish to squander even a second of the short time available to us.

Nik was off on his own, doing the things that an adventurous boy on the cusp of manhood does when set free in a strange city. Louise and I were trying to find a way to take best advantage of our time while avoiding the debilitating afternoon heat. Many of the tourists had retreated to shops and cafes, eating meals they did not want, buying souvenirs they did not need. Others sat in piazzas or wandered into museums and churches, where the cool darkness offered blessed counterpoint to the overwhelming heat.

Louise was looking to me for answers. After all, I knew the city, and she did not.

"We should go to Santa Croce," I said. It is a beautiful marble-fronted fourteenth-century cathedral that sits at the back of a broad, gracious piazza. I remembered it fondly from my time here thirty years ago, when I had chanced upon a concert being given beneath its great, cavernous vault. That evening, sitting beneath the crypts of Michelangelo and Galileo, listening to the grand expansive strains of Mahler's Second Symphony, was one of the most memorable experiences of my life. I could think of no better place to spend a sweltering summer afternoon than in that beautiful cathedral that had affected me so deeply those many years before.

We entered into its tranquil, echoing silence like people stepping from a desert into a forest glade. The space was overwhelming, the cool quiet a blessed sanctuary. We wandered from sculpture to painting to crypt to window, trying to absorb the beauty and monumentality of all that it presented.

Now and then we would catch the edges of a talk being given by a tour guide, or stop to wrestle with the Italian descriptions written on plaques near the famous works. But understanding was not what we were after. We wanted something that reached out and touched the heart, something that quickened the spirit and returned us to our ordinary lives enriched and enlightened.

Soon Louise and I, too, parted ways, each moving among the works at our own pace, seeking a place or a moment that touched some private place in our own spiritual yearning.

I could see her across the way, head craned or nose burrowed in her guidebook, seeking a pathway into meaning. I wandered up to Donatello's beautiful relief of the *Annunciation*. It was near here that I had sat during that transfiguring concert many years before.

The work has a stunning delicacy about it. Donatello took the iconic medieval pose of an angel kneeling before the standing Madonna and invested it with human emotions. The angel holds up one hand and smiles an enigmatic smile that seems to say, "I have a secret to tell you." Mary draws back in surprise and disbelief and places her hand across her breast as if to gasp, "Who, me?"

It is a well-known story, told often in literature and art. But at Donatello's hand, it became a spiritual moment, made soft and gentle by a man who understood and could voice the secret movements of the human heart.

I had never been touched by this work before, even though I had known it well and had passed it almost daily during my time here three decades ago. In those days I had been looking for something more heroic, more masculine, and had paid it little notice as I made my way across town to sketch from the great, struggling figures of Michelangelo's *Slaves*, so noble in their struggles, so titanic in their spiritual quests. But now I marveled at this gentle, intimate work that sits so quietly among the heavy masculinity of Florence's solid, heroic sculpture and architecture.

After standing before it for several moments with something close to reverence, I moved farther up toward the altar to look at the frescoes of Giotto and the other works that this magnificent cathedral contained. But my heart kept being drawn back to Donatello's *Annunciation*.

Finally, unable to shake the memory of those two figures sharing that moment of joyful intimacy, I gave myself over to its lure and returned to stand before it again.

There was the Madonna, almost disappearing into the shadows, drawing back gently, like someone given a gift she neither expected nor deserved. There was the angel, herald of good tidings, presenting his message less as an announcement than an offering.

I turned to find Louise, hoping to call her over to share in the beauty of what I had found. But she was far across the nave, staring up at a work of her own discovery.

In that moment I realized what it was that had changed in me since I had last walked through this great cathedral thirty years before.

In those days I had been young and hungry and obsessed with the pursuit of God. Spiritual truth was something hidden in the far reaches of understanding, something to be hunted down with reason and philosophy and theology. That was why Michelangelo's *Slaves* had so captivated me — they were figures struggling against the bonds of their own limitations. This *Annunciation* had been too quiet, too passive, to ever catch my attention.

But now, in this cool cathedral, I saw with different eyes.

Now the short gasp of the Madonna, frozen into a moment of stone, seemed just right. I understood that gasp; I understood that astonishment at the impossibility of life's miracles and mystery.

I glanced again at Louise, the wife I had never imagined. I thought of Nik, a miracle of our own creation, walking among the street vendors, trying out the rudimentary Italian of which he was so proud.

Yes, I thought, it all makes sense. I am no longer like the *Slaves* of Michelangelo. I no longer have to struggle, to do battle, to hunt and search for spiritual truth at the far reaches of faith and understanding.

My life is simpler now, gentler now. Like this gentle Madonna of Donatello's *Annunciation*, I am more than willing to be surprised by God.

The world is not something that happens to us;
we are something that happens to the world.

THE VISIT

For they all contributed out of their abundance,
but she out of her poverty put in all the living that she had.

— LUKE 21:1–4

The English streets were cold that night, colder than they should have been for that time of year. Mists rose up from the pavement, and the streetlights were shrouded in a spectral fog.

I pulled my collar tighter against the damp chill. It was still about six blocks to my home.

The boy surprised me — almost frightened me — when he stepped out. Something about foggy weather turns one inward, and I had been lost in private thoughts.

"Excuse me," he said. "Excuse me, sir."

He was young, not yet twenty, shabbily dressed, and not warmly enough for this chilling cold.

"Could you spare some change?" he asked. "I'm trying to get something to eat."

Like most people, I have become hardened to the beggars and panhandlers who wander the streets. I turn away, wave them off, sometimes even cross the street to avoid their intrusions into my life.

But this boy struck me differently. He was polite to the point of being obsequious, and there was an honest pleading in his manner.

I looked at him through the mist. He returned my gaze through sad and lonely eyes.

I started to shape a response — something about how there was no reason why someone so young and seemingly intelligent should be begging on the street. But then I stopped. There were many reasons why he could be on the street, and none were mine to judge.

A distant Gospel passage, as vague in my memory as the shapes in the fog, came floating back to me — "I was hungry and you gave me to eat." At this moment, it seemed less like a memory than a command.

I reached into my pocket for some change. There was nothing there. A bit less cheerfully, I opened my billfold, looking for a bill or two to give him. I had only a ten-pound note — almost twenty dollars.

He was watching intently. By looking for change I had given wings to his hope.

Against all my instincts and desires, I pulled out the ten and gave it to him. He looked at it with astonishment and thankfulness.

"Oh, Jeez, thank you, sir," he said. "You didn't need to —"

I waved him off. "You don't need to thank me," I said. "Just pass it on when you get a chance."

But the young man persisted. "No," he said. "I need to thank you. You have to let me thank you. It's all I have to give you in return."

His words took me aback. He was close to tears with appreciation.

"You're right," I said, taking in the full import of his comment. "I appreciate your thanking me. It makes me feel like I've done something important."

"You have," he said. Then he turned and ran off into the mist.

He had touched me deeply, but I thought little more about him. The cold was quickly overtaking me, and I turned my mind again toward home.

It wasn't until months later, after I had returned to America, that he came back into my thoughts. I was delivering a book to a friend who is seldom able to leave her house. Her body is failing, but her mind is sharp. She is always anxious for visitors, and always anxious to engage in conversation.

It was a busy morning, filled with many stops and responsibilities. I had little time to spend with my friend, though I knew that my visit was going to be the centerpiece of her day.

I arrived at her door, committed to making a quick and gracious exit.

She answered my knock almost instantly, as if she had been waiting, and gestured me warmly to the floral couch that sat against the far wall of her living room. I brought out the book and began to guide the conversation gently toward what I hoped would be a quick conclusion.

But she was having none of it. How was the family? Had the driving been bad? What did I think of the story she had seen on the news the previous day?

I gave short answers — polite, but without opening doors into other subjects she might be likely to pursue.

After what seemed like a respectful time, I readied myself to leave.

"Oh, just a minute," she said, and went off into her kitchen.

I pulled my chore list from my pocket and began shaping my route for the rest of the day. Already I was behind schedule.

Soon she returned with a plate of cookies, all arranged in a circle, each lying partially on top of the one next to it. In the center were two small chocolates.

"I made them this morning," she said. "It's a recipe I found in a magazine. Would you like some coffee or some milk?"

It was at that moment that the young man floated back to me out of the distant English mist. "I need to thank you. You have to let me thank you. It's all I have to give."

"Unless you're in a hurry," my friend said. She had seen my restlessness, and there was just a hint of sadness in her voice.

I settled back in my chair and shoved the list deep into my pocket.

"No hurry," I said. "I was just getting comfortable. And yes, a cup of coffee would be great."

TWILIGHT'S
VEIL

With our elders
we hold hands in time.

TWO OLD MEN

The years teach much which the days never knew.
—— RALPH WALDO EMERSON

Last evening we had some friends over for dinner ——
a husband and wife who teach history at the local
university, and a man who, in some measure, is
responsible for my decision to begin writing. He
is seventy-eight or seventy-nine, elfin in appearance,
but with a penetrating look that speaks of depths of
experience and understanding that I cannot begin
to fathom.

He was a child of the Holocaust — an Austrian Jew who, as a child, was taken by his mother to England to escape the spreading darkness of Nazism. He grew to manhood a wanderer on the earth, separated from his people and burdened with the dark knowledge that all he loved in childhood had died at Nazi hands.

He made his way to America and dedicated his life to serving others. He worked with the unions, and later among the Ojibwe Indians. He edited newspapers, built houses, taught children. He went where he was needed.

The other friends who were at dinner are wonderful historians. But they teach history; he embodies it. The passage of time is etched in his face and his memory, and is part of the fabric of his life experience. To understand his past is to understand America. Listening to him is to gain an insight into our world that can be attained in no other way.

Then, today, I was at the gym, and I struck up a conversation with the man sitting next to me in the locker room. He was old and sagging, but, like our dinner guest, he had an immeasurable depth in his gaze. He said that swimming was his therapy.

"I've been doing it for over eighty years," he said.

The math, though not exact, was easy: he had to be at least eighty-five.

He was pleased to talk with someone. Ours is a university gym, so most of the people using it are young, barely out of their teens. A sagging, balding old man whose skin is stretched tight and mottled over his skull is not a person with whom they would strike up a conversation. But I, being closer to his age, was better able to see past the age to the man himself.

As I listened to this man, I thought of our friend from the night before. In both of these men there is a wealth of knowledge and experience. But neither of them looks like Bertrand Russell or Arturo Toscanini. They just look like old men. And because of that, they are seen as elderly rather than wise.

But there is a wisdom that comes with age. The old have walked the path we tread. They have seen the landscape through which we are traveling. They have felt our passions and known our dreams, though perhaps in different shape and in different measure. In their eyes we can see our future. In our eyes they can see their past. In some fundamental way, they know the place where we are going.

The look I saw in the eyes of both those older

men in the past two days was a look of deep compassion and understanding. They understood something about me, just as I understand something about the hopeful, headphone-wearing twenty-year-olds in that gym. It is knowledge unspoken, but it is knowledge, nonetheless.

They also know that few will seek them out. They have accepted the fact that few will ask them to share what it is that they have come to understand. Their time has come and passed; the younger generations want little more from them than reminiscences.

I was honored to speak to both these men. I hope I showed them proper respect in our conversations. I hope, too, that I was listening to them for what they can teach me about life, not merely for what they can reveal as witnesses to the past.

For each touched me deeply. In their presence, I felt both judged and understood. It was as if their eyes, still bright, saw something I myself could not see. Their gazes gave me silent comfort, as if to say, "It's all right to be where you are. It is exactly where you ought to be."

It was the kind of comfort that I hope to give my son as I see him moving through choppy waters — a look of understanding that says, "You are not alone."

We live so strongly within the boundaries of our own experience. If we long for anything, it is usually for a time past, when we were younger, stronger, better looking, and not yet so bound by decisions we have made.

We seldom long for a future where our bodies are less but our spirits and insight are more. Yet, that future is there. It is in the eyes of those who have lived longer, seen more, and come closer to a resolved understanding of their place and purpose on this planet.

I feel better as a man, better as a person, and filled with a new sense of challenge and responsibility for having encountered those two old men. Their mortality, so close to the surface, has touched me in some deep and irreducible part of my own being.

I feel observed and, in a strange way, renewed. They have given me the gift of their witness and the blessing of their understanding.

May I take that gift, learn from it, and find a way to pass it on.

May I take that blessing and bestow it on my son, on other young people, on all those who come behind me, thinking they are discovering a world that has never been seen before.

*At the edge of our emotions
life approaches prayer.*

THE CONVERSATION

My whole silence is full of prayer.

— THOMAS MERTON

I met Ralph in midlife. It was my wife's second marriage, and he was not sure what he thought of getting to know a new son-in-law. The first had been good enough for him, and he looked with suspicion on anything that was a product of divorce — a practice for which he did not have a great deal of respect.

But slowly I had won his friendship, sealing it on the night we sat at his favorite bar drinking beer while watching a hockey playoff game.

But now he could watch nothing. The years of hard work and hard living had gradually sapped his physical strength, slowly reducing him from a gruff, robust man to a fragile, bedridden invalid who spent his days lying in an almost comatose state in my brother-in-law's spare bedroom.

It had been a difficult decision. As Ralph's physical capabilities had waned, we had all done what we could to keep him in his home, and when that was no longer possible, we had moved him first to a group home, then a nursing home, where he had sat all day staring vacantly into space with nothing to wait for but his meals and the occasional visit from his family.

My brother-in-law, a good and caring man, had been unable to endure the sight of his father ending his days in lifeless rooms bathed in sickly, pale half-light, and had chosen to move Ralph in with his family. Now Ralph spent all day in bed, unable to talk, unable to sit up, unresponsive, almost unconscious. The children and my sister-in-law treated him as one of the family. They would come in, say hello, ask him how he was doing, and try to bring some brightness into his life, not knowing if anyone remained inside the shell of the man who had once been the rock at the center of the family.

Louise and I live two hundred miles away, so we would see Ralph only on our infrequent visits. We, too, would go in, say hello, and make small talk. But we, too, were confused and uncomfortable, wondering if we were playing at some kind of dark charade by having one-sided conversations with a man who might not even be present to the words we were saying.

Yet one day, spurred by an offhand comment by my brother-in-law about how he left the radio on because he knew how much Ralph had liked to listen to ball games, I made an unlikely decision. Instead of just passing small talk in the emptiness of that silent bedroom, I pulled up a chair and sat down by Ralph's side.

I began slowly.

"I don't know if you can hear me, Ralph. I don't even know if this makes any sense. And if you can hear me, I surely don't know what it is that you are going through."

I looked at Ralph's impassive face to see if there was any response. His skin was ashen, and his skull, pressing through the flesh, made him seem like he was made of stone.

"I figured, though, that you never hear anything of what's going on, and I just wanted to tell you a little about how your family is doing."

I told him how his wife, Mary, now had her own apartment and how we were all helping her in every way we could. I told him about each of the grand-kids, what they were involved in and how they were doing in school. I talked to him as a man talks to an-other man, trying to assure him that the lives he had tried to give to each of his children were bearing good fruit, and that the family he was leaving behind was filled with promise and hope.

It was a strange conversation, both hollow and intimate, for I was speaking as a man speaks in the quiet of his own heart when he recounts his own life to himself in a fumbling effort to make sense of the things he has done. All I could hope is that the calm tones of my voice and the earnest offerings of my heart were somehow reaching past the emptiness in Ralph's eyes to touch him, like half-heard music, in some distant place where his spirit still ranged free. In the kitchen, I could hear the clinking of glasses and the shuffling of plates. It was time to finish up; the table was being set for dinner.

I reached over to put my hand on his, as I always tried to do whenever I entered or left. There had been no movement, no sign, no awareness that I had been there at all. His hand felt cold and hard, as though it had already been claimed by death.

"You know, Ralph," I said. "It's okay to go. You did well. The family is fine. We're all carrying on."

I stood up to leave. But as I stood up, I caught the momentary glimmer of some moisture in his eye. Then I stood there, mortified, gratified, as a tear coursed gently down his lifeless cheek.

Finally, my wife's voice, calling me to the table, brought me back to the land of the living. I took my hand off his and stepped toward the door.

"I'll see you, Ralph," I said into the silence.

Then I walked out to join the Sunday family dinner with its laughter and commotion and good-hearted conversation.

But my heart was not at that table. It was in the silent room, only a few steps away.

And as I joined with the family, brought together

around a common meal, I prayed, in my own clumsy fashion, that Ralph could hear the clinking of the glasses and the rise and fall of laughter, and that in them he could find some comfort, as one finds comfort in the rolling of a distant sea.

NIGHT'S
EMBRACE

It is good to weep together
as it is to sing alone.

THE CIRCLE

There is no death. Only a change of worlds.

— CHIEF SEATTLE

Dark woods, far from any city, on the day of the first snowfall of the year. The wind lashes cold and heartless through branches that reach skyward like broken fingers. November is not a good time to be buried. There is no feeling of redemption or resurrection anywhere.

I am gathered with a group of people in a Quonset hut on the Red Lake Indian Reservation. There are probably sixty of us; I am the only white person here. We sit in folding chairs on a cold, concrete floor. The casket stands open in front of us, veiled with blue lace.

The man who is being buried had just turned thirty. He was once a student of mine. He had been a lonely and troubled boy, seldom in class. I remember him most for the time I got him out of jail. He had no family or, if he did, they no longer claimed him. He had stayed with aunts and friends and other people's grandmothers, and in abandoned houses and on roadsides.

He was a hustler and a con man with a grin as big as the world. But on the day I had bailed him out of jail, he had been a small and frightened boy, though by the time I dropped him off in front of a house where he thought he could stay, he was full of his old bluster and swagger — a bravado and braggadocio as hollow as an echo.

I last saw him only a few weeks ago. Years had passed, and he was now a man with two children and a wife. He still had the con-man smile, but there was a new gratefulness in his eyes. He had known the sorrows of an abandoned childhood, and he took his parenthood seriously.

"I'm working for Red Lake Builders," he said. "Three years now," as if holding a job was a day-by-day accomplishment, like an alcoholic staying sober. "I just made foreman."

I clapped him on the shoulder. "Good work," I said. "You've done all right for yourself."

He smiled. I was still the teacher, and my approval made him proud.

But I was the one who had felt most proud. I had seen a boy become a man, a lost child gather a family around him and claim his place upon the earth. Perhaps my touch had played a part in this. And even if it hadn't, the wound I had carried in my heart for him was healed.

But now the wound is open again as I sit in this cold Quonset hut, so full of cigarette smoke that my eyes burn, watching as one more of my students is buried before his time.

It is a strange and alien setting and, despite my friendship with some of the people, I feel out of place. The great arcing building is hollow and empty. It has the feel of a converted repair garage for heavy equipment. The walls are chipped fiberboard, rising white above the cold concrete floor. Dim fluorescent lights flicker from the ceiling.

There are no windows, no warmth, just the high cold illumination of these spectral lights, and below it, against one of the curved walls, the casket, with the body shielded from clear view by that veil of blue lace.

Beside the casket, brown Masonite folding tables are set along the wall. A few sympathy cards are spread out across their surface, along with a sparse scattering of flowers purchased at a grocery store and placed in makeshift vases. In the corner near the door, wooden boxes and packing crates and a rolled-up tumbling mat are shoved against a foosball table, making a haphazard pile of objects that will be pulled out again as soon as the funeral is over.

On the far end, against the flat back wall, stands another line of Masonite tables covered with plastic food containers and cooking pots and battered aluminum cake pans wrapped with tinfoil.

In the center, beneath the cold fluorescent lights, rows of folding chairs sit facing the casket, on which the mourners sit quietly, talking among themselves, smoking cigarettes, and drinking Styrofoam cups of coffee and cans of Coke and Mountain Dew.

A slow, low dirgelike prayer is being chanted by the head man, who is seated in the front row. It is almost inaudible — part recitation, part song. Occasionally, low laughter rises up from somewhere among the folding chairs. Children run across the floor, their footsteps echoing in the hollow emptiness of the Quonset space.

Except for my red jacket, it is all jeans and gray hooded sweatshirts and black nylon baseball jackets with logos of powwow groups and alcohol rehab programs. Men wear baseball caps with insignias from logging companies and auto repair shops. Women wear jeans and sweatpants and heavy, shapeless jackets.

A few of the teenage girls have on floor-length out-of-style velveteen dresses bought at secondhand stores or left over from some long-forgotten school dance. They walk around in heavy shoes, whispering to each other and chasing after their toddling children.

At intervals I don't understand, the dirge stops, the shaking of a rattle begins, and we all stand. The chant takes on a singsong edge, moving from high to low, before returning to its inaudible murmur as the rattle stops and we all take our seats again.

Every few minutes the door to the Quonset opens and the cold winter light shafts in as someone enters or leaves. Smoke curls to the ceiling and floats like captured fog around the humming lights.

The dirge continues, as does the standing and the sitting and the rattling. At a certain signal, the chanting stops, and an old woman who is assisting the head man stands up. She walks with a hobble, like someone who has one leg shorter than the other. Her pale hooded sweatshirt is covered with coffee stains.

She gestures us to the food tables, and we all line up to fill our paper plates with wild rice and macaroni casseroles, pieces of venison, gum drops and hard candies, fry bread, white bread baloney sandwiches, potato chips, Rice Krispie bars, and Oreo cookies.

At the end of the serving table we each stop and scrape a bit of food from our plate into a green garbage bag propped up inside a cardboard box, in order that the spirit of the deceased may have food to accompany him on his journey to the afterlife. I tear off a chunk of fry bread, and push a bit of baked beans in with my fork. An old man across from me drops pinches of tobacco in the bag; young children pour in offerings of Mountain Dew and Pepsi, then look up at their mothers to seek their approval.

We mill and gather. I see some of my other students, now grown to men and women, with their families or alone. We talk a bit, then return to our seats where we each eat quietly. There is a heavy silence to the gathering, punctuated by an undercurrent of casual joking and laughter. It is the solemnity of close friends; you cannot suppress the sense of community that lies at its core.

When the eating is over, the old woman stands up. "I want you to come up now," she says. "The friends and relatives first. If you got glasses, you got to take them off so he can recognize you. If you got a little kid, or if you're pregnant, you don't come up, because we don't want their little spirits to get scared. Then the family, I want you to come up last. You put some charcoal on your forehead. The rest of us will be up here to support you."

My student's mother, whom I had never met, is weaving in her chair. Some people put their arms around her. A young girl goes up behind her and begins to braid her hair.

One by one, we file up. A circle of ferns marks the floor around the casket. The old woman pulls back the blue lace veil. The body is clothed in a leather jacket and a baseball cap. People stand over the corpse, touch the hands, kiss the cold lips.

When it's my turn, I place my hands on my student's gloved hands and try to bring a memory of his smile into my mind. I can hardly recognize him through the embalming. He died in a car accident, and his face is a grotesque, inflated caricature; skin stretched flaccidly over balls of wadded cotton. On his cheeks are perfect circles of bright red rouge, as if painted by a clown or an old lady with a dime-store makeup kit.

I pay my respects and move off to stand near the boxes and the foosball table and the tumbling mat.

When all the guests have filed by, the family gathers around the body. It is the same as at all funerals when those closest to the dead are faced with the closing of the casket. I look away, trying to give them the privacy of their grief.

But many of the mourners have stayed close by. They gather around the family in a tightening circle, literally holding them up. They lift the wailing mother by her arms and move her back to her chair. Quiet hugs and whispered words are shared.

The old woman gestures to some of the younger men. They pick up their chairs and move to the front of the room. One of them brings in the powwow drum. It is about three feet in diameter, made of a wooden frame with animal skins stretched taut over each surface and held to each other by zigzag patterns of hide and sinew.

"They're gonna play four songs," she says, "for the four directions."

The drum is placed in a frame made from two-by-fours, protected on the bottom by a piece of old carpet. The twelve men — one for each moon of the year — pull their folding chairs into a circle around the drum.

The old woman faces us. "The drum is a circle, and the circle is strong," she says, "strong in all four directions. Any of you who have lost someone, you come up and stand in a circle around the drum. It is okay to cry. The circle is strong. It can take your grief."

Slowly, everybody in the room begins to file up. We have all lost someone.

We gather behind the drummers, expanding the circle, until it is five or six people deep.

The lead drummer starts a low beat, like rhythmic distant thunder. The others join in, first almost inaudibly, then gaining in strength. The lead singer holds his throat, as if pulling on his Adam's apple, and begins a high-pitched ululation. It is a wordless ancient song, one he learned from the elders or heard from the birds or remembered one morning when he awoke from a dream.

The other drummers pick up the melody, following it, mimicking it, accentuating it, but keeping their voices always in unison. One takes the lead, then another, lifting their voices high above the others.

But always they return to the common voice. It is a young voice, a strong voice, for they are young men, strong men, in their twenties and early thirties, doing what their ancestors have done before them, what they themselves were taught as young boys. The small children crowd around, hoping to learn what they, too, will someday be called upon to do.

The singing increases in power and pitch. The black animal skin mallets hit the drumhead in hypnotic unison, each coming in from a different angle, reaching not quite to the center, rising and falling, almost in a blur. Like the voices, one will rise up, go higher, hit harder, then the others follow.

Soon they are all hitting harder. The rhythm is stronger. The drummers' faces become contorted and strained. The drum begins to bounce wildly in its wooden frame. In the circle, women are moving, bobbing, in an echo of an ancient dance. The men put their arms on their wives' shoulders. The little children cling tightly to their mothers' legs.

The singing rises almost to a wail. The drumming takes on a dark and frantic edge, full of anguish and brutality.

And soon, without warning, the grief begins to pour forth from all of us, one by one — our private grief for mothers and fathers now dead, for friends lost, for children buried in tiny graves, for this young man, dead too soon, and his young children left fatherless, for four hundred years' heartbreak of a people, for pets lost, dreams forgotten, lives poorly spent. It is not one grief, it is all griefs, come together, and none can resist its common pull.

Tears flow. Muffled sobs come from the chests of the old men. The young men stiffen and wipe the corners of their eyes. The women weep and hold each other, the children cry and stare up at their mothers. None of us can escape, and none of us wishes to.

Amid the Coke cans and the cigarette butts and the half-claimed rituals reduced to gum drops and potato chips in green garbage bags, and the casseroles made with commodity foods, and the people arrived in cars with broken windows and doors held shut with bungee cords, we stand as one in the stark dim illumination of this Quonset hut, pouring our grief onto that drum.

The drummers are almost frenzied now. They attack the drum as if it were alive. It bounces in its frame like an animal trying to escape. I fear it will shatter under the rain of their frantic rhythmic blows, just as I fear we will all collapse under the weight of our common grief. But it endures. We all endure.

Then, slowly, one by one, the drum strokes soften. The lead singer keeps up his haunted ululation, but the others withdraw their voices, one at a time. The drumming continues, but with ever-diminished intensity, like thunder retreating, until it is distant and gentle, almost like an infant's heartbeat. The voices still, and the song becomes as soft as a lullaby.

We all stand, shaken, in the circle. Our breathing stills, our hearts quiet. One by one, we file back to our chairs. We sit with eyes down, lost in our private thoughts. We are once again separate beings.

The service goes on, filled with rituals to which I have no entry.

The casket is wheeled in circles; the head man offers Ojibwe prayers. The old woman says, "The spirit is still with us until we let him out that door. Then he will be gone."

The head man chants. The people stand in silent witness while the sacred pipe is smoked so the spirit can be set free. Then the casket is carried out and placed in the pickup truck that will carry it to the grave that the men dug this morning.

I follow slowly behind as we make our way to the burial ground. Up ahead, I can see the pallbearers huddled in the back of the pickup, standing vigil over the casket. The sleet is blinding; the wind off the great lake is cutting and vicious.

At the gravesite the head man takes charge. He

begins his prayers in earnest. People gather around the grave in a circle, while the young men shout instructions to each other and lower the casket into the hole with ropes.

The head man points to one of the children. "Now you kids put the flowers in." The children file up one by one. Some stare into the grave as they drop their flowers. Others throw them from a distance, as if they are afraid to get too close.

"That's good, you little ones," he says when they are finished. Then he nods to the rest of us. "You fill it in now," he says. "You all put some dirt in. Even a handful."

There are four shovels. My student's friends grab them and begin shoveling with the same frenzy with which they beat the drum. It is as if they have to get the casket covered before their grief escapes. Some jump in the hole and begin tamping the dirt around the edges. Others get down on their hands and knees and push the wet, muddy clay in with their hands. One by one we all take our turn, throwing the cold, wet earth into the rapidly filling hole.

Someone gives me a shovel. I toss in dirt until another man takes the shovel from me, then I get down on my knees and begin pushing the mud in with my hands.

The wet earth seeps through the knees of my pants, up the cuffs of my jacket. It soaks my gloves and freezes my fingers. We work together, the old men, the young men, the mothers and daughters, the tiny children and the grandmothers. Some throw just a handful; others shovel with a fury. We get the casket covered, then stand with the moist, rich earth caking our hands and clothes and knees and faces.

We have buried him. We have placed him in the earth.

The head man directs a few young men to cover the grave with a sheet. The ends are held down with dirt, then the whole surface is covered with plastic flowers.

The sleet has turned to snow. People pull their jackets tight around them. The head man smokes the pipe, sends the smoke in the four directions, down to mother earth, up to father sky.

"Well, that's it," he says. "*Miigwech*. Thanks for coming."

I wander back to my car with the earth wet and heavy on my hands. There has been no meaningful ending, but somehow it all seems right.

A little boy, no more than six, is standing by my

car. I recognize him as one of the children who had crowded around the drum.

"Hi," I say.

He looks away.

"You going to be a drummer, too?" I ask.

He brightens and nods his head.

It is thirty dark miles back to my home. The roads are icy, and the forests deep. I look at my hands, and the clay that covers them — the clay of my student's grave, the clay of his people's ancestors, the clay that will one day take their bodies and the bodies of their children and their children's children.

I cross the reservation line, back into familiar country. Back into America. Something passes from me, something I cannot understand. But it slips away as surely as the spirit of my student slipped away when they carried his casket through that Quonset door. It is an understanding, deeper than memory, as deep as the grave we filled, as deep as the land on which we have been standing.

For a moment, in a cultural setting as alien and inaccessible to me as the stars, I had been part of the drum, where what strikes in one place reverberates through us all.

And I think of my student, gone before his time, and the girls in their thrift shop dresses and the men in their baseball caps, and the children and the elders and the old lady with her coffee-stained sweatshirt, and the mother, returned to claim her child, and the young men, steel-eyed and purposeful, drumming their departed friend's spirit to the beyond.

And I remember the young boy, staring up at me with hopeful eyes, and how we had all, for that brief moment, held each other up, sharing a common grief made strong by our common embrace.

And the old woman's words rise up once more: "The circle is strong. It can take your grief."

What more do any of us ever need to know of healing, and of love?

CODA:
TRAVELER'S REST

All religions, all this singing. One song.

— RUMI

It is late November — the end of a long journey. I am staying in a monastery for the night before returning to my home a hundred miles away.

I lived for a time in places like this when I was younger. I know the power of the long accretion of silence, and the great, wheeling ritual of the liturgical hours and the liturgical year.

Like a man returning to the land of his birth,

some part of me wishes to stay, to give myself over to this familiar spiritual embrace. But this is no longer my world. It is the streets, the people, the birds, the animals, the trees — the joys and struggles and passions of everyday life — where my life now brushes against the sacred and my spirit finds its strongest voice.

But on this night it is the great peace of the eternal that washes across me, and it gives me an easy rest.

I wake to the bells, walk silently to morning prayer. The slow cadence of the monks' morning chants calms my spirit; the great arching space of the monastery chapel echoes the peace back on me, amplifying it, enveloping me.

The memory of another great arching space comes, dreamlike, into my thoughts — the Quonset in which my student's funeral had been held. And that other ritual with its other circle, far different from this great circle of liturgical times and seasons, rises up before me.

Once again, I am surrounded by people in black. But here it is monks' robes, not logging jackets and heavy sweatshirts. Once more, the common voice is raised, with one taking the lead, then another. But here it is the voice of monks intoning the Gregorian chants, not young men singing the powwow songs of the birds and the ancestors.

How different these two worlds are, but how much the same, each reaching out to the Great Mystery, the Creator — the One, the Being, the Presence we so clumsily call God. Each claiming a ritual fashioned and honed over centuries, each raising a voice in common prayer.

The chants wash over me with their ineffable peace, just as the powwow drum enveloped me with its urgent grief. Again, the power of the common heart carries me to a place I could not easily go myself.

When the prayers are over and the monks silently file out of the chapel, I walk alone along the echoing aisles. The vaulting space rises above me, lifting my eyes, lifting my heart.

Off to the left I see a small sanctuary illuminated by a single candle. It beckons me with its secret intimacy.

I enter its dark confines. A single kneeling bench faces a carved, wooden Madonna with the Christ child sitting on her lap. Their faces flicker in the wavering light cast by the solitary candle. They seem pensive, meditative, almost alive.

It is an ancient carving, worn and weathered, devoid of color or polychrome. It was shaped by humble hands over a thousand years ago, and it has the spiritual presence of a faith that did not try to find the human in the divine so much as to offer divine consciousness as a message to the human.

It has an almost Buddhic presence. The Madonna and her child sit upright, motionless, with eyes closed, the child's hand raised in benediction. Their drapery is heavy and straight, like fluting on a column. There is no movement in their gestures, no movement in their expression. They are creatures of the eternal, not creatures of time.

I kneel before them and stare silently at their impassive, peaceful faces.

They are utterly self-contained. They do not reach out to me with human emotion like the surprised Madonna of Donatello's *Annunciation*. I have to go to them, to try to find the peace they possess, as one seeks the peace of a mountain. The presence of God blows through them like wind through a hollow reed.

Once more I feel the presence of the spirit, as I had in the voices of the birds, the man with his dancing kite, the gratitude of the young girl, the dark rhythms of the powwow drum — each showing me its pathway to the sacred, each opening to a different room in the mansion of God.

I stay for a while, letting my thoughts give way to silence. Then I walk from the sanctuary into the pulsing rhythms of the day. I am once again part of life's raucous, joyful noise.

I make my way slowly from the cities through the pines to my home on the edge of our distant northern lake. It is evening when I arrive.

The wind is blowing music through the trees. The moon is beginning to claim the sky with its muted crescent presence. One by one the stars are piercing evening's darkening veil.

A loon cries out over the lonely lake.

It is a sound far different from the birds in the eaves at Oxford — more private, more haunted, less immediate and intimate. It seems the perfect heralding of the oncoming night.

I walk quietly toward my home to await the

arrival of my family. The wind in the trees brings memories of the chants of the monks.

Today, like all days, has been good. I have done what I could, tried in my way to be an instrument of God's peace.

Tomorrow, like the sunrise, will come soon enough. It will crease the dawn with promise, and the birdsong will sing its anthem to the coming of another day.

ABOUT
THE AUTHOR

Kent Nerburn holds a PhD in religion and art. For many years he worked as a sculptor of religious imagery, with major works in such diverse settings as Westminster Benedictine Abbey in Mission, British Columbia, and the Peace Museum in Hiroshima, Japan. He also spent several years working with the Ojibwe Indians of northern Minnesota, helping to collect the memories of the tribal elders.

He is the author of the highly acclaimed books *Simple Truths, Small Graces, Make Me an Instrument of Your Peace*, and *Letters to My Son*, as well as the award-winning *Neither Wolf nor Dog: On Forgotten Roads with an Indian Elder*. He is the editor of *The Wisdom of the Native Americans* and *The Soul of an Indian*, and he recently published the ground-breaking work *Chief Joseph & the Flight of the Nez Perce*.

He lives with his wife, Louise Mengelkoch, and his son, Nik, on a lake near the Canadian border in northern Minnesota.